OWL

OWL

Rebecca Stefoff

HOUGHTON MIFFLIN BOSTON • MORRIS PLAINS, NJ

California • Colorado • Georgia • Illinois • New Jersey • Texas

Photo research by Ellen Barrett Dudley

Cover photo: *Peter Arnold, Inc.*, Roland Seitre

The photographs in this book are used by permission and through the courtesy of: *The National Audubon Society Collection/Photo Researchers, Inc.*: Anthony Mercieca, 2, 10, 19, 20 (bottom), 21; Steve Maslowski, 6-7, 12 (left), 13, 14 (top); Jeff Lepore, 9; Jany Sauvanet, 14 (right); Gregory K. Scott, 15; L.W. Richardson, 17 (bottom); Craig K. Lorenz, 20 (top left and right), 25; Manfred Danegger/OKAPIA, 26-27. *Animals Animals*: Joe McDonald, 7; Truay Unverhau, 8 (left); Zig Leszczynski, 11; Leonard Zorn, 12 (right); Breck P. Kent, 16; Muzz Murray/Oxford Scientific Films, 17 (top); Alan G. Nelson, 18; Mark Chappell, 22 (inset); Richard Kolar, 23; John Gerlach, 24; Michael Leach, 32. *Peter Arnold, Inc.*: Carl R. Sams II, 8 (right); John Cancalosi, 14 (bottom); Bios/Klein-Hubert, 22.

Houghton Mifflin Edition, 2001

Printed in the U.S.A.

ISBN: 0-618-05984-9

456789-B-06 05 04 03

For Zachary

screech owl

eastern screech owl

There is a bird that flies when the moon is high. Like a shadow, it glides silently through the night forest.

It is the owl.

eastern screech owl, New England

great horned owl, Canada

Owls spend the day in nests and hiding places. In the late afternoon they come out and look around them. Then, in the soft gray dusk, owls spread their wings and take off.

great gray owl, Canada

All owls are hunters. Some eat insects, birds, or fish. Most owls eat little animals like mice. Even in the dark, an owl's big eyes can see a mouse scurrying through a field below.

burrowing owl

long-eared owl

The owl drops down and clutches its prey with powerful claws. Then it flies up into a tree to eat. When you find small balls of bones and fur on the ground, you'll know that an owl has been eating on a branch above you.

barn owl and owlets

screech owl and owlets

Mother and father owls spend a lot of time catching food for their hungry young ones. They bring mice to the nest and teach the young owlets how to use their claws and beaks.

The parent owls' job isn't easy. Some have twelve owlets to feed! But most owls raise four to six young each year.

Baby owls are covered with soft, fluffy, white feathers. As the owlets grow, some of their feathers will turn brown or gray.

young barn owls in nest

snowy owl, Michigan

spectacled owl, American tropics

great horned owl, Arizona

barred owlets

Owls live in all kinds of places. An owlet's home might be a snowfield near the North Pole or a cactus in the desert or a tree in a tropical rain forest.

A family of owls might live in a tree or a barn near your house.

barn owl

The barn owl sometimes makes its nest in the corner of a barn. Most barns have mice, and barn owls love mice!

But barn owls don't *always* live in barns. They nest in other buildings, especially old, empty ones. Barn owls have even been found in big, busy cities.

Outdoors, a barn owl might look for a hole in a tree trunk. A cave in the side of a cliff also makes a fine place for a nest.

Do you know how to tell if an owl is a barn owl? Most owls have round tan or gray faces, but the barn owl has a white face shaped like a heart.

young barn owls, England

barn owl cliff nest, Utah

great horned owl

Whoo-oo-oo. Whoo, whoo, whoo.* The hoot of the great horned owl echoes over the fields and forests as evening falls.

The great horned owl is one of the biggest owls in the world. It's about twenty-two inches tall (56 centimeters). Pretend one is standing next to you. How much taller are you?

The long-eared owl looks like the great horned owl, but it is smaller, only fifteen inches tall (38 cm). Its "ears" aren't really ears. They're just tufts of feathers, like the horned owl's "horns."

long-eared owl

elf owl, Arizona

elf owl nesting in saguaro cactus

pygmy owl, Montana

saw-whet owls

The world's tiniest owls live in Mexico and the southwestern United States. They're called elf owls, and they're not even six inches long (15 cm). The elf owl in the top pictures on the other page is bringing a tasty cricket back to its nest in a cactus.

Saw-whet owls and pygmy owls are also small American owls. Pygmy owls are fierce hunters. Sometimes they attack birds that are bigger than they are—and they win.

snowy owl watching over nest (inset), *Greenland*

snowy owl

The snowy owl lives in the cold northern parts of the world. There are no trees or barns here, so the owl lays its eggs on the ground.

In the winter, the northern lands are covered with snow. In its coat of white feathers, the snowy owl is almost invisible.

Burrowing owls got their name because they live in burrows—holes or tunnels in the ground. Sometimes twenty or thirty of them live together in one big burrow.

burrowing owls, California

burrowing owls, Colorado

Burrowing owls are also borrowing owls. They like to borrow holes dug by prairie dogs or other animals. But if they have to, they can dig their own burrows with their long, strong legs.

Eurasian eagle owl

Drifting through the trees as quietly as a cloud, the owl sees and hears everything that happens on the ground.

Is that a rustle in the grass? The flicker of a tail? Down drops the owl.

At dawn the owl returns to its nest and closes its bright eyes. It waits for another sunset, another mouse, another night.

A QUICK LOOK AT THE OWL

There are about 150 different species, or kinds, of owls in the world. They are different from other birds because they have round heads, flat faces, and eyes that face forward. Most owls are active by night, although they can see well in daylight. Owls can turn their heads three-fourths of the way around: this lets them look behind them and gives them a very large field of vision. Their keenest sense is hearing. Even in total darkness, owls can locate their prey by sound.

Here are six kinds of owls, along with their scientific names and a few key facts.

ELF OWL
Micrathene whitneyi
(mee crah TAY nay WIT nay ee)
World's smallest owl. Measures less than 6 inches (15.25 cm). Lives in canyons and hilly regions of Arizona, California, and Mexico. Nests in small holes in trees or saguaro cacti.

WHITE-FACED SCOPS OWL
Otus leucotis
(OH tus loo COH tis)
Adults are about 12 inches tall (30.5 cm). Called by some bird lovers the most beautiful of all owls. Several kinds of scops owls live in Asia, Africa, and Madagascar, a large island off the coast of Africa. They are among the world's rarest owls.

NORTHERN SAW-WHET OWL

Aegolius acadicus (ee GO lee yus ah CAH dee cus)
A small owl, measuring 8 inches (20 cm). Found in central and northern United States and southern Canada. Lives in dense forests or wooded swamps. Name comes from its call, a raspy sound like a saw being sharpened. Also whistles.

BURROWING OWL

Athene cunicularia
(ah TAY nay kew nih kew LAH ree yuh)
Averages 9 or 10 inches tall (23–25.4 cm). Has long legs, unlike other small owls. Often seen running across ground. Lives in American Southwest, Mexico, and South America. Pairs or groups nest in ground, usually in holes dug by other animals.

SNOWY OWL

(Nyctea scandiaca)
nik TAY uh scan dee AH cuh
Heaviest owl in North America. Adults are 20 to 27 inches tall (51–67 cm). Lives in far northern North America, Scandinavia, and Russia. Rarely seen south of British Columbia, Canada. Flies during daytime.

EURASIAN EAGLE OWL
Bubo bubo
(BYEW bo BYEW bo)
World's largest owl. May measure 30 inches (86 cm) from beak to tailtip, with a span of 80 inches (2 m) across outspread wings. Can kill prey as large as a small deer or a fox. Lives in Europe and Asia.

Taking Care of the Owl

Many kinds of owls have managed to live side by side with people. But some owls are in danger because the places they live, such as forests and prairies, are disappearing. Owls also become sick or die when they eat mice or rats that farmers have poisoned. We need to protect owls. They are a vital part of the web of life in many parts of the world. And without them, our fields would be overrun by mice.

Find Out More

Epple, Wolfgang. *Barn Owls.* Minneapolis: Carolrhoda Books, 1992.

Esbensen, Barbara J. *Tiger with Wings: The Great Horned Owl.* New York: Orchard Books, 1991.

Guiberson, Brenda Z. *Spotted Owl: Bird of the Ancient Forest.* New York: Henry Holt, 1994.

Sadoway, Margaret W. *Owls: Hunters of the Night.* Minneapolis: Lerner Publications, 1981.

Sattler, Helen Roney. *The Book of North American Owls.* New York: Clarion Books, 1994.

Storms, Laura. *The Owl Book.* Minneapolis: Lerner Publications, 1983.

Index

Rebecca Stefoff has published many books for young readers. Science and environmental issues are among her favorite subjects. She lives in Oregon and enjoys observing the natural world while hiking, camping, and scuba diving.

barn owl